Persuading Plato

Books by Ioana Petrescu

I say…, in New Poets 5 series, Friendly Street,
Wakefield Press, Adelaide, 1999
Fumigated, Ginninderra Press, Canberra, 2001

Books edited by Ioana Petrescu

Friendly Street Poetry Reader 26, editors Ioana Petrescu and
David Adès, Friendly Street, Wakefield Press, Adelaide, 2002
*Heart of the Matter: An Introduction to Eighteen South
Australian Poets*, editors Ioana Petrescu and Naomi Brewer,
Lythrum Press, Adelaide, 2004

CD (project manager)
Adelaide 9: The poetry of the city, featuring nine Adelaide
poets, produced with the support of Arts SA, 2003

Ioana Petrescu

Persuading Plato

Acknowledgements

Island (Then it was time to say something again); *Southerly* (Gnomes, lecture); *Asiatic* (His collarbone, Luck 1, Editing); *Journal of Australian Studies* (Luck 2, Migrants, (in)certitude, The next-door neighbour); *SideWalk* (Tear gas); *Vernacular* (Geography); *Friendly Street Poetry Readers* 26, 27, 28 and 29 (The moon, always, Silly moon verses, Convalescent ward, Becoming, Tanka for a cat, Expecting, Camping); *artlook* (pickled tongue); *Artstate* (Tanka for a cat); *Beyond the shimmering* (Sculptor); *Famous reporter* (Trinkets); Radio 5UV Adelaide (Early afternoon); Poetry CD: *Adelaide 9: The poetry of the city* (Luck 2, (in)certitude)

Persuading Plato
ISBN 978 1 74027 742 6

First published 2012
Reprinted 2016

GINNINDERRA PRESS
PO Box 3461 Port Adelaide SA 5015
www.ginninderrapress.com.au

Contents

Foreword

In her poem 'Camping' Ioana Petrescu details the way in which friends of hers in Australia have to take a holiday in the Outback to experience the hardship (the cold, thirst, hunger and lack of mod cons) that was a daily reality for her in Romania before she made her escape from it. In another poem, she wonders if anyone in Romania now misses her generation, the thirty-year-olds who, though they were too young to stay and too old to migrate, did pack their suitcases and leave. We may ask in turn whether her generation misses Romania. They would have been fools to stay in a place where life was insupportable, given half a chance to migrate to a place which promised a better life. Yet, however much ease in Zion may now be pleasant for the poet, she may find her poetry craves to feed off those earlier, darker times when, as a memorable line of hers puts it, she (quite literally) counted the days by the nights.

This is not to make some facile contrast between Romania and Australia. It is that the experience of the passage from one to the other throws into relief the disparities or paradoxes that were evident prior to it and become more evident after. In her opening poem Petrescu casts her mind back to an encounter in a train in Romania amid the turmoil following the fall of Ceauşescu. An intellectual, she is engaged in a conversation with a miner, as respectful of her as was that iconic Australian plumber of hers some readers may recall from her volume *Fumigated*. Yet she is aware that the previous year, during a demo in a Bucharest street, the miner could well have beaten her up or raped her. There is a clear class and gender disparity – but also a sense of disparity in the recognition that a year can change everything. Encounters, as well as mineshafts, can be seen in a new light.

Petrescu follows up a sequence of poems casting back to the Romanian Revolution with a sequence on houses she has known in Australia. In one of these poems, 'Early afternoon', the poet is shown over a house where she had once lived. The taste of the new owner is quite different. The house is and is not familiar. As in the previous poem, Time (whether past or present) is seen to have its dislocations no less than places (whether here or there). It is this awareness of disparity that provides Petrescu's poetry with its tension, brings it into being.

This sense of disparateness is further reflected in the diverse forms to be found in each of the opening sequences. Was the Romanian Revolution conducted in a series of succinct haikus? Do the Australian seasons turn like a succession of geisha girls? The collection explodes in a multiplicity of directions, plundering in a playful post-modern way the fabulous riches of, among others, the Arabian Nights, Oscar Wilde and Marin Sorescu. It is all positively surreal. And why shouldn't it be? If an Australian friend goes on holiday to experience the sort of deprivation the poet once lived with on a daily basis, then shouldn't we conclude that life under Ceauşescu was one long holiday?

In a further poem, 'Afternoon at Buon Giorno's', Poetry with a capital P, elegantly sitting drinking lemon, lime & bitters, remarks that her interest now is in the lyrical stance of the ordinary. To which her interlocutor, Mephistopheles, replies, 'Bullshit.' Should Poetry sell her soul to this devil? Of course she should – but only if he is a less whimsical figure than the neo-Gothic Dracula Bram Stoker ascribed to the poet's native Transylvania.

John Drew
Cambridge, UK

Tear gas (Romania, 1991)

I'd rather be with my own thoughts,
        but this man feels like talking.
It's winter and we carry our social classes
        in this second-class compartment.
The train is not heated,
        we're still recovering after the revolution.
Craving warmth,
        I'm wearing my grandmother's fur cap.
No one minds except me –
        in fact, I'm often envied for the warmth of the dead otter.
He's wearing a heavy winter coat thin at the collar and elbows.
        He hardly ever sees the light, he tells me – he is a miner.
I look through my own poverty every day in the daylight –
        it's as transparent as his winter coat's elbows.

He was in last year's riots. Miners marched upon the capital city
        to demand decent work conditions.
There's power in numbers.
        And in wooden clubs.
They got carried away –
        smashed windows and doors, beat up policemen,
declared war on intellectuals, raped women in miniskirts
        'because that's what they want, don't they?'
Tear gas
        was the answer of the newborn democracy.
'Y'know, ma'am' he says, 'I used to have ulcers.
        All those irregular meals in the shaft at odd hours.
But after the riot my ulcers was cured.
        D'you think it was the tear gas?'

I feel solidarity with this man,
        but know that last year if he'd seen me
wearing a miniskirt in the university street,
        he and his mates would have beaten me up.
'I don't know,' I say, 'I don't know if it was the tear gas.
        How does it feel to work there in the shaft?'
'I've got used to it,' he says,
        'and we've got neon light.'

I live in the daylight and the cold with a dead otter's fur on my head,
        and right now I'm sharing a train compartment with a man
who would have beaten me up had he met me last year
        before he got rid of his ulcers.
I look him directly in the face.
        His eyes aren't swollen and itchy any more. Mine are.

Migrants

1.

Twenty kilograms per person, says a voice on the phone
and I look at my suitcase. A few clothes, shoes,
two books – I ripped off the covers to make them lighter.
The other books I own will have to stay behind.

I also own a few dreams. They don't cost money
and weigh nothing.
The dream about stardust heavy on my shoulders…
The dream about words on paper forever…
I'll always carry these with me.

The dreams in my suitcase, the things on my mind.
I'm weak, I'm scared.
We're only given, my mother says,
the weights and burdens we're able to carry,
so I kiss her goodbye and take my suitcase.

2.

The purple elephant, the grey elephant, and Tiny Elephant.
Lego bricks, more Lego bricks,
fairy tale books, colour-in books, how-to-fold-paper books.
The Yogi-Bear-Friend badge and framed Diploma.
The sledge, the ice skates, the rollerblades, the bike,
the little doctor kit, the little gardener kit, the little mechanic kit,
and drawings, many drawings.
Twenty kilograms they say. You need to choose.

My son arrives in Adelaide with Elly, the grey elephant,
some Lego bricks, two books,
and the light toys courtesy of the airlines.
For years, my son will sleep with the elephant of his choice,
building dreams out of Lego bricks.

Revolution Scenario, Romania 1989

Haiku

Molten fear flows
through transparent arteries,
sets the veins alight.

Asthmatic rifles
wheeze and cough up solid spit
that sticks to the walls.

People chant slogans
by day, then hang their prayers
in the twilit sky.

Women buy candles,
save water in big pots,
lock their screams inside.

Words hang on men's lips
like wet cigarette butts,
stain their breath and tongues.

Do you miss us?

After the 1989 Revolution Romania experienced one of the most significant migration waves in its history.

Do you miss us – the generation
who took our suitcases and left,
those of us who were then thirty?
We were many, too young
but also too old and complicated –
too late to stay, too late to migrate.

Is there a void where now
the forty-year-olds are missing,
or, as soon as we left, the space was filled
by waves of generations, by the tides of many –
the ocean of genetics regenerating gaps
wave after wave after wave?

Camping

For Mike

'Each year we go camping
in the Flinders Ranges,' says my friend,
'no water, no toilets, canned food –
the dirt, the joy of it.'

I wake up in the cold – electricity
needs to be rationed.
Water needs to be rationed –
it comes through pipes
twice a day for two hours.
I save up drinking water,
water to wash my face,
and in the bathroom, in the tub,
I have what I call 'my indoor pool'.
The bathroom is cold.
I freeze when I go to the toilet.

'Our kids had a shock,' says my friend,
'when they had to go to the toilet
in the bushes, in the cold –
does them good, roughing it, city kids.'

'Just imagine – no shower for nearly a week,' he laughs.
Just imagine – warm showers
if you're lucky. Finish quickly
so you have time to go to the kitchen
and save drinking water.

'Just imagine – canned food from the car boot,' he says.
I boil an egg on the pale flame –
gas is supplied at dawn for an hour.
Seven eggs per month is the ratio.
When I finish them
I eat canned food.

'Do you enjoy camping?' he asks,
and I suddenly realise that's what it was
back home before the '89 Revolution –
forever camping.

pickled tongue

language an olive on my pickled tongue,
the jar suspended on the shelf of (in)difference.
cry in a language, laugh in another, add pepper and chilli.

odd other, different tongue, buds pink as prickly roses,
as pickles tickling taste buds.
laurel in brine crowns forgotten fulfilment.

Luck

Kneel in front of this fountain –
the angels carved it with their wings, poured water
to quench your thirst with holy luminous drops
in which you can see your reflection –
pear-shaped, heart-shaped, tear-shaped – until it bursts.
You throw in a coin for luck. It says on the sign
that if you give a coin to the waters your life will flow
smoothly, love will bless your heart, you'll see ideas
with your pineal eye – but why would life flow, you ask,
if its model is a carved fountain surrounded by a pool
of stagnant water?
And the question falls flat on the pavement
and is picked up by a pigeon
who thinks you're just another tourist
who feeds it crumbs.

Early afternoon

Always accessible, rarely revisited,
the houses I lived in occupy spaces in my memory
as they were when I had to leave them.

The house in Lawn Street has flowers now bordering the front lawn
as if moles had dug out tunnels swallowing the green
to make way for patches of pansy-yellow, pansy-purple
and kitsch-pansy-blue.
The peach tree with the sunniest peaches I've ever known
was cut, and the perfumed vine was cut too –
it used to live entwined with the branches of a frangipani tree
grapes incongruously hanging heavy among scented flowers.

The host is happy to have me over, to show me
what money could do to the house I lived in –
the hall is adorned with a Persian rug
and a bare-breasted bronze statue;
the floors in the living room have been polished,
the old carpet was peeled off and thrown away.
A wooden cuckoo with a brassy call announces the time.

They cut down the fruit trees – the peach tree at the front,
and the pomegranate tree, the loquat trees, the pear tree at the back.
Near the fence, where the neighbour's cat chased sparrows,
there's a vegetable garden; no cats are allowed here.
The lawn is orderly, tidy, freshly cut
and will soon be cut again.
No parrots stain the backyard sky with their loud colours –
they just sway on the branches of the pomegranate tree
in my memory.

I thank my host for the perfect Earl Grey tea
and leave through the hall of the house I lived in.
From outside I can hear the wooden cuckoo
announcing the hour.

Amateur in the leafy suburbs

As my life gets better
the owner of the corner Deli
and the hairdresser
suddenly understand my accent.
However, I'm asked to repeat what I said
when they learn I'm just renting.

As my life gets better
the landlady drops by just to say hi.
She's dressed to the nines
and smells of French perfume –
my previous landlady
used to smell of French fries.

As my life gets better
I have two bathrooms, two showers,
two toilets,
so I can feel safe.
Established.

Open inspection

The house opens its baggage for inspection.
Shy thoughts are chased away in the daylight,
a radio covers street noise, and incense adds a layer of scent
to the odour of smoked grass and sewage.

Drawings, beads, wind chimes,
off-street parking, near-city crammed living.
'You need to put in a good offer,' smiles the agent,
and I'd love to help this house regain its lustre
but I can't.
The house pulls down its shutters,
embarrassed that it opened up to a stranger.
We're both embarrassed. It failed, and I failed.

*

The auctioneer's words envelop me, scare me
the discourse flows persuasively
right in the middle of this suburban yard.
I like you, I tell this house,
I love your red brick walls, high ceilings,
big yard and well-groomed flower beds.
I don't put up my hands.

*

This house is full of advice.
The rosary next to the cookery book gives you recipes,
the workbench in the garage emits inaudible noises –
the ethics of work done previously.
A huge granite slab in front of it
is carefully planned as a 'random feature'.
'Your thoughts,' says the house
'will have to fit within the perimeter of this square lawn,
and your imagination will need to follow the contours
of the grey granite slab.'
I elope from the 'openness' of this inspection
and look up through the gnarled branches of a gum tree.

*

> A woman must have money and a room of her own if she is to write fiction.
>
> Virginia Woolf, *A Room of One's Own*

Words and thoughts drive me out of the room of myself
I have occupied each and every corner
with parts of vocabulary.
I'm cluttered with words.
There's a spider web on an idea in a corner,
perhaps the angular corner, the angular cornerstone
of my words and thoughts that
drive me out of the room of myself,
of this room,
this house.

*

This wilted flower bed costs money
the cracks in this wall cost money
this broken cement drive costs money
the half-roof with no gutters on one side costs money
and you can have the goldfish in the brittle weed grown pond
for money.

The worst-house-in-the-best-street scenario costs money.
The bank loan, the mortgage, the passport to stability –
my person and my remaining years of working life
are all measured in money.

*

I saw her when driving past the house I was thinking of buying, her floral blue-and-white gown stark against the flashy Real Estate signboard. She walked down the path towards the end of what was still her garden. She stopped, looked at the street, silver-white hair combed neatly, her face wrinkled, her floral gown so clean and proper.
A developer outbid my offer.

Geography

Let's meet.

I'll give you my exact location,
its coordinates, longitude and latitude.
I won't tell you where my soul lies –
you need to discover that as part of
the 'great geographic discoveries' game.
I'll give you some hints: a glance, a smile –
you know, the usual stuff.

Conversation also helps. Well, it's true
that my thoughts indicate the East
and yours indicate the West,
but then we've still got
two more cardinal points
where we could meet.

The moon, always

Little girl – sweep the floor with a broom
and half of the moon will be yours.
If you wash, cook and sew well
the whole moon will shine through rooftops,
shadows will dance on fences,
your first kiss will come down with a star
and will gild you into holy matrimony
like a golden moth in the globe of a lamp,
in the light of the moon,
always the moon.

Good girl – moans and moon go together.
Your belly will swell, your breasts will swell,
milk will flow from your breasts
like the milk of the stars on the Milky Way.
Part your legs for the seeds, part your legs for the fruit,
and the moon will be there stuck to your window.
Is it truly the moon?
Always the moon.

Nice girl – sweep the floor with a bunch of moon-rays,
cook stars with rice for dinner,
pull the thick blanket of the sky
over your body,
over your eyes –
thick wool, thick blanket,
sweep the floor,
dance with the moth,
bleed with the moon –
always the moon.

The next-door neighbour

1.

My best friend loved the Beatles, Elton John, mucking around with electronic parts and repairing old TV and radio sets, although he always failed maths and physics. When we were little he used to catch wasps and dissect them to show me the sting. From the safe distance of his first floor window he would squirt passers-by with water to make me laugh.

His mother was beautiful – blonde, blue-eyed, disillusioned. His father was handsome. He drank and chased other women. They often quarrelled and then my friend came over to our place until they finished yelling at one another. 'Can we play outside?' he used to ask. My mother liked him and always agreed, so we went outside. He knew hidden places where builders had abandoned huge slabs of stone and concrete. Thick snow covered the yard so we climbed on the slabs and jumped, landing in the snow facedown. There was no time there – only space and the joy of falling on smooth snow, our faces red with cold, our clothes full of tiny icicles. My mother would find us. I would get hot soup and he would get yelled at by both of his parents.

2.

One day he came around to say hi and tell me to leave those books for a while because he had something to show me. 'Can we go to the forest?' he asked and my mother said, 'Go, you need the fresh air,' so we left the city streets behind and went to the forest. There was no one there, just trees, bees, flies, birds. I found that lonely, but he thought it was beautiful. We arrived at a small pond in the forest and he proudly showed me the water.

'See, salamanders,' he said, 'they've just hatched! Look at those colours: black-and-red, black-and-orange, black-and-yellow.' Shiny salamanders swam in the pond flashing their colours in sun rays filtered by fir trees and water. 'Shall I catch one for you?' he asked and I said yes, so he caught a big salamander in a translucent plastic bag. Those eyes blinked. Dinosaur lids slid upwards, covered the eyes – didn't like me. 'Do you want it?' my friend asked and I didn't want it. I thought it was happier in its pond and I couldn't take that look in its eyes with me. He put it back in the pond and asked if I was thirsty. I was, so he looked carefully in the moss and found the herb he wanted. 'Eat this,' he said, 'it's sour and you won't need water until we reach the spring.' I trusted him so I ate that sour herb and all of the wild berries he picked for me. We reached the spring and we drank fresh cold water. 'Do you like it?' he asked and I liked it. 'Then why don't you say so?' he said, so I said again that I liked it.

We reached a plateau and I was scared – you could see the town there in the valley and it seemed very far down but he said the earth wouldn't slide because of the rocks, so I sat down. The town was there like a map and he showed me all the historical buildings – I knew how to find my way in their museums and archives, he knew how to spot them from up there.

We lay in the grass, watched the clouds move and talked about the partners we'd meet in ten years' time and marry. I said I wanted to marry an intelligent man and the looks were not important. 'Could he look like me?' he asked and we laughed. Well, no, he couldn't look like him, what a thought. He said his wife had to be blonde like his mother. He'd never yell at her, he said. They would have four kids and he wouldn't yell at them either. Then we just lay in the sun and watched the clouds.

3.

I met him again years later. He repaired our TV and showed us photographs of his blonde wife and two kids. He had a job but they were struggling. 'Did you show her the salamander pond?' I asked and he said he didn't know what I was talking about. 'Did you feed her sour herbs and wild berries?' He then seemed to remember. 'It was the place,' he said, 'where you felt you could gather the city in your palms and put it in your pockets. And you also felt as if you could touch the clouds.'

'Did you like that place?' he asked while I was filling the cups with coffee. 'I did.' 'So why didn't you ever tell me?' he said, and then left. 'Why has he left?' asked my mother looking at the untouched coffee. 'Perhaps because of salamanders and clouds.' My mother gave me a puzzled look. I sipped at my coffee and said, 'Forget it.'

Cold

I wrestled with the cold that morning.
Dew jazzed up the lawn
and the tree at my porch
was gleaming with drizzle.
My neighbour's cat was just returning home
tired and shivering,
but her ears stood up bragging.

Convalescent ward

When I was on display
pinned to a hospital bed
by drip-needles stuck into my arms
I bowed to the pain
then tailored two patched butterfly wings
from a white hospital gown.

In this game of chess

there's just one player: me.

I opened up with white and advanced two squares.
After I lost a few white and black pawns
I learned how to use the remaining ones, but then
one of my black horses started playing up.

Somehow I managed to keep my towers.
I also used my bishops once or twice –
they ran diagonally across the chessboard
beating the clock, enjoying the pleasure.

Halfway through my game
I started to build fortresses around kings.
I tend to take more time now
before making any new moves –

I pick up one ivory piece, hold it,
warm it up in my palms,
then let it play with the ebony ones
trying not to give myself a checkmate.

Owned

The canary brought him a lot of joy – it hopped and fluttered through the big cage, it ate and then drank water from a shell shining with thick layers of mother-of-pearl. It whispered, trilled, whistled and every now and then it sang at the top of its high clear voice.

The owner thought the bird would look better in a gilded cage, so he took the cage to a jeweller who covered it in 24 carat gold. The canary hopped and trilled as before, but the owner's pleasure was even greater. He drew the curtains, opened the window and let the sun shine on the golden cage. What if the canary were golden too, he thought, so he took the bird to a jeweller who gilded its beak and legs. The canary shone as bright as its cage and when it hopped around its legs caught the sun in their gold. When the bird drank water, the beak glistened and the owner's heart jolted at the sight of such beauty. However, he'd noticed that the bird was mostly whispering and whistling now, the trills were rare and they occurred usually at sunset.

One day while watching the sun rays lighting the cage he decided to take the bird to the jeweller's again. One by one the feathers were covered in 24 carat gold. Now, when he let the sun in, cage and bird nearly caught fire – flames of light in pure gold lit the room and enchanted the owner's heart, mind and soul.

But one morning, when he took the cover off the golden cage he was shocked with disgust – the bird had died with its beak in the water-shell. Golden feathers covered the cage floor and the canary had nothing left on its tiny body but the finest down which had been shielded by feathers and couldn't be covered in gold. The beak glistened in the water, but the gold on the legs had started to flake off. A dead bird cannot sing, hop or glisten, so the owner carefully peeled off the gold from the beak and legs and threw the bird in the garbage bin.

Then he bought a solid-looking tortoise and the jeweller assured him that gold sheets would adhere well to the shell-surface, would not flake, and the tortoise wouldn't even notice the difference while eating, drinking and strolling through the golden cage.

Window

Purple vibrations beneath the brown crust,
promise of flowers,
this side of the window, inside –
petunias.

Twisted tilted twigs alive
with intimate life,
outside –
geraniums.

City grey, urban flutter,
hatched with a street directory in their genes,
streets viewed from above, from windowsills –
pigeons.

Tanka for a cat

Sumptuous grey fur
covers his sagacity,
claws sharp underneath –

rat liver for his master
placid joke and offering.

Geisha seasons

Tea, conversation
and chopsticks. Feelings blossom,
never reach full bloom.

Does she quiver when
you touch her? Does your summer
make her beautiful?

Before they settle
on the cold ground, autumn leaves
hang onto sun rays.

What makes winters meet?
Nothing, now. Seasons follow
their usual sequence.

Behind curtains

Motto: But when it was midnight Scheherazade awoke and signalled to her sister Dunyazad who sat up and said, 'O my sister, recite to us some new story, delightsome and delectable, wherewith to while away the waking hours of our latter night.' 'With joy and goodly glee,' answered Scheherazade, 'if this pious and auspicious King permit me.' 'Tell on,' quoth the King who chanced to be sleepless and restless and therefore was pleased with the prospect of hearing her story. So Scheherazade rejoiced; and thus, on the first night of the Thousand Nights and a Night, she began her recitations.

from Richard F. Burton, *The Arabian Nights*

Scheherazade

King Shahryar is nearly asleep – his black eyelashes
lazy wings of birds covering the eyes of the horizon.
The lightest touch on his eyelids would awaken him,
he'd want me to finish the story,
the ending of this story a threat to me – an end.

The thrill of recognition not so much heard as remembered,
shadows move within,
possibilities are protean, eroticism is displaced by words,
suspended in narrative –
the King succumbs to sleep, vulnerable to possibility.

He's asleep. It's late at night, nearly dawn,
I can touch him now, lightly, gently –
his body my desire, his desire my curse,
my curse – my story.

The Scribe

Scheherazade's stories fill the King's mind,
search his memory, sweat in his bed.
'When she's been slain,' he thinks, 'her words will vanish,'
and starts missing her stories already.

Thoughts turning into words, turning into stories,
saving leaves of time burdened by the early autumn's weight,
yellow with jealousy, burgundy with desire.
Words pulsating in arteries, descending through veins,
setting blood in motion through their significant, signified reality,
a no-man's land of connotations, denotations –
the way of words.

The King calls the Scribe. He arrives with scrolls of parchment,
brown ink, gold dust and elegant egret feathers.
He sits behind a curtain,
his worthiness measured by the accuracy of writing the words
of another storyteller, his gift of storytelling never seen.
His wrist designs masterful loops,
pins to wooden fibres Scheherazade's each breath, his words mingle with hers,
intimately entwined in ink and parchment –
the King will never be able to see through this new betrayal.
The Scribe caresses Scheherazade's words with an egret feather –
fathers them into writing.

The Scribe's story

Friend, listen to what I have to tell of the truth,
Stay with the red wine and a silver body;
Whoever made the world could not care less
About the pair of moustaches you are and the beard I am.

Omar Khayyam, *Ruba'i* 228

Shadows behind curtains – words turned into moans.

The Scribe fears for his life; Scheherazade's story
has been a mere parable tonight – a joke,
she has now other ways of pleasing King Shahryar,
therefore the Scribe makes up and writes his own enchanting tale.

Merchants, sailors, porters, thieves
drip their sweat on the Scribe's parchment, conjure up a world
that thrives and pulsates beyond the palaces of Kings and Queens,
of Wazirs and their daughters.

The differences in topic, rhythm and style
are proof of the narrator's versatility,
literary critics will say hundreds of years later.

Behind the curtains the King is pleased –
Scheherazade will be graced through royal decree
with a ruby for each moan
and an emerald for each ecstatic spasm.
And she will live for yet another day and night.

Scheherazade's thirteenth story

Jinni escaped from the bottle of thoughts
twist around your head a turban spun of nightmares.
Take the delicate hand of the Princess
in your own blue hand – smoke and sapphire.

She has big eyes, brown
like the cobra watching your riches,
but unlike the cobra
no venom flows through her teeth –
she's pale and light and you want her.

You fly above the desert. Shiny snakes rear their heads,
you pick them up and twist them around your head.

Jinni made of smoke you wish for a body – your own,
so you can possess another's body.
The Princess is yours and isn't. Trying to make love to her
is trying to go beyond your image in the mirror –
you feel nothing but desire, she feels nothing but fear.

Outback haibun

No ghosts in this town.
Dismantled houses – a place
left behind. Like hope.

A solar-powered phone booth, a pub, a tourist shop – no ghosts.
Uncelebrated, unremembered,
they left the desert to its inconspicuous life.
A lizard unfolds its spinal fan, two eagles guard the highway,
three kangaroos have spilled their guts on the asphalt,
a sheep has the entire horizon to itself.

For miles the lookout
looks at no people, the plain,
the saltbush, the sun.

Eftpos. Expensive paintings, prints, beads, emu products,
greeting cards, more paintings and prints, silver and tin baubles.
There's a tourist shop in the desert. No ghosts.

Geometry

In
whichever
direction
a
bird
flies
it is still not parallel with anything
sky
the
across
cut
still
will
it

Song in gnomic verse for a mediaeval minstrel

Wolves must be in packs   bears in caves.
Brides must be in beds   gold on their hands.
Warriors carry the swords.

Song must be in drinking halls   with loud laughter and chatter.
Wind must be in the sails   rain must fall upon the earth.
Dragons guard the future.

Hidden in riddles   is the music of the harp
the journey overseas   the never seen treasures.
The minstrel is alone with the song.

Writing

I.

Writing is an alley cat eating fish bones
from trashcans of the everyday.

Writing is both the harmonious thoughts
and the hard and round scattered sheep droppings.

Writing is a scalpel cutting through the flesh
of naked reality.

II.

Writing is setting pen on paper
because the mind pushes the hand
images turn into words
and setting pen on paper lends them corporeality.

III.

Writing is praying in solitude to a sheet and a pen
hoping that someone
who is physically and metaphysically removed
from you, your sheet and your pen
will hear you.

Silly Moon Verses

The moon is a shiny butter dollop.
The poet melts it in the black pan of the sky.

*

The moon is a round Swiss cheese.
The poet sifts his imagination through it.

*

The moon stayed late last night.
The poet smears makeup on its purple rings.

*

The moon has just had breast implants.
The poet worships her silicon.

*

The moon is stuck on the top of a pole.
The poet basks in its lantern light.

*

The moon is reduced to a sickle barely there.
The poet mows metaphors with it.

*

The moon wishes it could climb down from its pedestal.
The poet fixes it in place with superglue.

Expecting

I feel that poem's heartbeat, it's a presence
nurtured through neuronal synapses
like an egg nurtured through the umbilical cord.
Thoughts flow towards it
pump the oxygen of discourse,
words are arranged grammatically
to match an internal DNA that is now being encoded.

Hands

The silence is in my left hand –
my right hand writes the poems,
gets fascinated, finds the good words.

The left hand is quiet. It holds the notebook
and all of the thoughts that remain untold, undone,
unspilt on the page.

Editing

That poem was made of grit and mud,
it was grubby in its unformed syllables,
earthy in its unmouthed words.

Its blistered language was infected
by long-festering thoughts, its lines
wrapped around like stuck rotting bandages.

I ripped the crust from the poem's wounds
and recited it loudly, rolling it on my tongue.

I licked the poem clean verse by verse, then watched it heal,
its form now clear and pure for others to judge.

Lecture

empty lecture theatre door ajar, a neon light on
someone has written formulae on the whiteboard
the sense eludes me I look at the empty chairs
no eyes look back to the podium I stand
observe the minimalist furniture, carpeted stairs
chairs with little mobile tables attached
in an hour I'll have to perform after so many years
I still feel the same emotion *trac de débutante*
leave the world at the door of the classroom
my teacher had said be there only for them
and I am; I perform they applaud once, I lectured in a place
where instead of applauding they knocked on their desks
the sound surprised me it was still the sound of success
only different find a friendly face in the audience
and talk to those eyes it'll seem
like you're making eye contact with everyone, she had said,
there are always people who want you to succeed
who wish to justify their presence and time in that theatre

Then it was time to say something again

For Rick

Hemingway has his own breed of men,
he wasn't one of a kind – those men who love words
and the sea, boats, hard work with their hands
up to their elbows in stinking bait,
rocking to and fro on cold waters.

*

He had a ponytail. Cut it off when the kids grew up –
made him realise it had to go.
The pipe and ute stayed.
He's got his place at that table, with the boys,
he's one of the boys. He drinks the wine
of conviviality in that rough-elegant way,
the nonchalant way of Hemingway's lads.

He lets me into some of those secrets:
'The fisherman I know
told me not to tell the others that I'm an academic –
just fish, sort and clean, that fisherman said.'

*

It's holiday – time for him to leave the books again
and clean fish guts, live a bush story,
look at the unpredictable, convivial trajectories
of stars above the campsite.

Somewhere by the sea, by a campfire redolent of bait and sweat,
Ernest talks to him and others about fish, boats, utes,
and the power of beautifully crafted written words.

Sculptor

He who planted moss on the rocks
had mastered pure green and moist
earthen scents hanging from the granite wall
where thinkers had stumbled against the void.

> *hard texture of the song of rocks*
> *split fragments of knowing*
> *knowledge sought and found*
> *echoes released by splintered wood at the foothills*

That forehead was already chiselled by thought –
geological strata appeared in maps of skin.
While singing the song of stone he turned body mass
into hubris cast in the shape of an instant.

Gift

Water and calcium mingle in lives of oysters and snails,
the spirals in their shells aspire to evolve into that last coil
reduced to a quintessential dot.
Minimalist colours create tasteful discrete designs
brownish-cream, yellowish-white –
the palette of French surrealist painters who thought the sea was a cradle
and Gaia, mother of all things, toned in ochre the days of shells.

Trinkets

1. Marble

Long hair flipped in a frozen moment
cold smooth breasts rounded by a chisel
milky white – stone hard
siren on the mantelpiece.

2. Glass

I know all about glass.
It fears the flight of birds,
the rhythm of hearts,
the inaudible thoughts
outside its translucence.

Light knows
it has to tap gently with its fingertips
so glass can let it undulate
with and within its frozen waves.
Light reminds glass
of the time when it was liquid –
blazing and glowing,
fearful of nothing but water.

3. Porcelain

Frightened pigeon in my cupped hands
hot coffee its throbbing heart
cobalt and gold on white as light as feathers.
I look through the brown eye of the brewed liquid.
Deep down I can read in porcelain the story of sand:
SiO2 in kaolin in water in heat.
Cup in my palms – sand in the form of birds.

Sketches for women

Shrewd little eyes assess me,
decide I'm no one important,
forget about me,
do the room,
smile at people who can make things happen.

*

Three kids, a husband, two cats,
a job, a house, friends. She creates her own space,
then generously engulfs things and people.
Anything can exist there –
even her friendship for me.

*

Men bow in front of her,
then whisper behind her back.
She puts on another year, wears it proudly,
plays the power game by no rules,
wins, then boasts,
attacks again – hard and fast.

*

'See, I didn't know sex could be fun
until I met *him*,' she tells me,
then reels off a list of the lovers she'd had –
all respectable men,
but with limp dicks and no technique,
according to her.

*

Round eyes, round belly,
all rounded
in the round house.

*

****
****

Self-portrait with stars.

Gnomes

I'm walking on the sand
careful not to fall through the hourglass.

*

I wrapped gifts in the silk paper of a moment – the ocean, the sky,
and a 17th century conquest map of my then non-existent self.

*

If words are clouds
is rain their discourse?

*

The garden gnome chased the concrete tortoise
while time stood still.

*

Perhaps poetry is the craft of creating certitudes
in ambiguous spaces.

*

If love were a cockroach, it would survive squalor,
sweet nonsense, and, presumably, atomic attacks.

*

The aberration of light refracted by fish scales sends myth into error:
I am seventy per cent water; the rest could be wings.

*

I wish I could fly, said the fish and turned into a flying fish
its scales and wings resplendent in the sun.

*

Could orange duck alleviate
l'ennui de la bourgeoisie?

*

I live in a shoe 'cos my house is so blue
and the poem jumped over the moon.

*

Kids catch ladybirds to release them and see them fly.
What if one day a ladybird chose to stay?

*

Ladybird, ladybird, scan a poem in one word –
say you're not a noble lady, say you're not a singing bird.

(in)certitude

> Plutarch's parallel lives are not paralleled by my life
> which keeps intersecting with other people's unparallel lives.

I wake up to a late-night TV commercial.
That dream again…I should stop working late,
coffee is not good for me, and I really need to do those dishes.
See – when you do the dishes you line up the cups and glasses
in rows. Parallel rows on parallel shelves,
clean glasses, clean cups. Orderly. Tidy.

So I do the dishes, make coffee, and sit at my desk
to write a long-overdue essay.

> The essence of postmodernity lies in the fact that there is no essence.
> 'Essence' is a determined notion delineating a certitude.
> There are no certitudes in a postmodern space.

Then, a chance meeting could be
the transitory intersective moment
determined by people's independent coming and going
their own individual ways…
Which, perhaps, might explain logically why my life
keeps intersecting with other people's unparallel lives.

Afternoon at Buon Giorno's

Poetry with a capital P was drinking a latte
at Buon Giorno's in Rundle Street
where cars and pedestrians
sweat a common urban cloud, a mist
like spray near waterfalls only thicker,
hardened by the heat
emanating from the bitumen below.
It's hot and perhaps a latte
is not the best drink for such weather,
so let's begin again.

*

Poetry with a capital P was drinking lemon,
lime and bitters at Buon Giorno's in Rundle Street
when Mephistopheles appeared
dressed in a T-shirt which said, 'My brother
went to Romania and this is all he brought me'.
He looked good and had a new deal:
he was interested in migrant poets
from new zones of conflict because, as we know,
the Romanian revolution was twenty years ago –
who would be interested to hear how scared I was then,
people need to know how scared other people are now.

So, like I said,
he sat down and asked me what I've been writing lately.
Well, I said, I'm interested more and more
in the lyrical stance of the ordinary,
in cadence and rhythm.
Bullshit, said Mephistopheles.

Poetry with a capital P sipped at her cold fizzy drink
and left the whole weight of the conversation
on Mephistopheles's shoulders – they were slender
but well-defined, manly yet beautifully shaped.
You still admire beauty
wherever you see it, Mephistopheles smirked.

*

Take three: Poetry with a capital P
and Mephistopheles in a sweaty T-shirt
asked me to wear a Gretchen dress
while asking Gretchen questions –

do we have to write about politics
do we have to write about sex
do we all have to do it in a fixed form

and other such questions
that hissed on hitting the hot bitumen
swirled through the air like mad balloons
and unsettled the passers-by of that city afternoon.

*

People looked at each other on that afternoon at Buon Giorno's
and shook their heads –
olives spelled elegant verses on pizzas,
cannelloni arranged themselves in stanzas,
there was a fresh metaphor in each foccacia
and drinks had layers upon layers.

Poem for my mother who died of cancer in 2007

I dreamt you with violets –
the kind from home with big round petals
their colour and fragrance so clichéd
that they felt familiar, close
almost as if
you were

His collarbone

I haven't thought much about the family grave
but I have often wondered how that peony flower
broke through cement. I can see now,
it's firmly anchored to the sides, beneath the headstone.
My mother's coffin just fits underneath.
The priest pours oil on it, I don't know why,
I haven't been to church in years.

There are two bags on the side of the grave.
These are your grandmother's bones, he says,
and these are your father's.
First time I see my father after twenty years,
a bag of bones. I shouldn't faint, it's him, and yet,
all I can see poking through the bag
is this delicately curved white collarbone.
I wonder how he could carry me when I was little,
on his back, if his white bones were all that delicate.
He should've drank more milk, I think,
the priest pours oil over the bones,
I don't know why and what it means,
I haven't been to church in years.

Priests and doctors.
The first poke at your soul, my father used to say,
the second at your body. So he smoked some more,
brown nicotine designs mapping the hands
he waved reciting verses from Baudelaire.
They know nothing, he used to say,
coffee puts blood pressure up, and vodka puts it down,
and if one drinks both at a time
the perfect balance is achieved, he used to say,
and drank more coffee, balanced out with vodka.

My mother's coffin's lacquered and has leaves carved in the wood,
she used to love flowers and leaves.
The priest lowers the bags of bones back in the grave:
one is my grandmother, the other is my father.
Now they are both together at my mother's feet.
The priest pours oil, I don't know why,
I haven't been to church in a while,
and I can still see my father's collarbone.

Thoughts

Place: If the everyday is an oyster
I've found my world.

Poem: Words huddled together
waiting to be shaped by the warmth of a moment.

Love: Glasshouse for emotion –
growing palm trees inside, while watching the snow fall.

Reserve: Oversized magpie strolling through empty space
in the afternoon heat.

Colours: Naïve art reproducing
naïve nature.

Words: Parts of me
on a journey.

www.ingramcontent.com/pod-product-compliance
Lightning Source LLC
Chambersburg PA
CBHW062200100526
44589CB00014B/1886